THE ALPHABET QUEST

ISBN# 1-930710-51-8
Copyright ©2000 Veritas Press

Veritas Press
1250 Belle Meade Drive
Lancaster, PA 17601

First edition

THE ALPHABET QUEST

— STORY —
NED BUSTARD

— ART —
JUDITH A. HUNT
CARLOS GARZON
& NED BUSTARD

Veritas Press

THIS BOOK IS DEDICATED
TO MY DAUGHTERS
CAREY ANNE AND
MARGARET ELLEN
—EACH A WORK OF ART.

NED BUSTARD

It was going to be a fun day at the art museum. Mother was excited. Father was excited. Even the baby was excited. But William was NOT excited. Not one little bit.

"Why are we going to an art museum instead of someplace fun like a toy store?" he said. He did not even look at the stone arch that went over the museum door like a rainbow. "We passed a toy store on the way here."

"Yes, we know," said Father. "You have reminded us of that fact several times. Art museums *are* fun and there is more to do here than in any toy store."

Father paid for the tickets and the family went inside to see what awaited them.

Huge statues of winged lions and bearded kings looked down on the little family as they entered the museum's Ancient Art wing. William thought he heard a clanking noise behind them. He turned to look, but there was nothing behind him but a boring suit of armor. A golden glittering sarcophagus made the whole family gasp in delight. Even the baby cooed. William had to remind himself that he would rather be in a toy store.

"This place is going to make me die of boredom," he grumbled.

"I used to live in a Kingdom. What is a Boredom? Is a Bore higher or lower than a Duke?" a tinny voice echoed.

The boy peered into the shadows but saw nothing but another old suit of armor. "Who said that?" William demanded.

The tinny voice went on wondering. "Or, if you can die of Boredom, is it perhaps some sort of a disease? Nay, worse! Would Boredom be a hideous creature?"

The voice seemed to be coming from inside the old suit of armor. It sounded like someone talking into a metal pail. It went on, "I have seen many wondrous strange things while I have lived here, but nothing which would inflict a mortal wound. Have you encountered Boredoms before? I once fought and killed a huge

ogre. Perhaps we might join together and engage this foe?"

William was startled, but curious. "What is your name?" he asked. "Where did you get that terrific suit of armor? Would you lift your visor so I could see your face? And what are you doing here?"

The metal suit bowed with flair and said, "I am Percival. I was crafted for the son of Sir Roger of Bellingham. It was he who named me for that famous knight of the Round Table. I do not know what you mean by wanting to see my face, but I would be happy to raise my visor."

He lifted his visor. Instead of eyes, nose, and mouth, all William

could see was the inside of an empty suit of armor.

"Aaaaaaaaaaaa!" screamed William.

Father and Mother turned around to look. Mother put a finger to her lips and said "Now William, you're supposed to be quiet in museums. Screaming is definitely NOT allowed."

Mother looked at the suit of armor. "Didn't we see a suit of armor just like that when we entered?"

Once Mother and Father weren't looking Percival continued in his tinny whisper, "Sorry lad, but grown-ups aren't allowed to see the museum's collection walking and talking like I do. They find it

very disconcerting, so the whole collection has agreed to stay motionless while visitors are here. But at night, we work to keep the artwork safe since the security guards can only be in one place at a time. Why just yesterday, the Assyrian lions scared away a brace of burglars. But beyond matters of security, it is simply a pleasure to get to walk around looking at the artwork in the museum all day."

"Looking at a bunch of old paintings and stuff doesn't sound like fun to me," said William.

"Well you see, that just goes to show that you are looking but not really seeing. Why, if you are truly looking, a painting or sculpture

will show you something new with each and every visit. Perhaps you would see this if we were to play a museum game together. Do you know your alphabet?

"Of course I do!" William shouted indignantly.

"What do you do, dear?" his Mother turned to ask.

"Er... nothing" said the boy. Even if it involved art, playing a game with a walking, talking, empty suit of armor sounded far more interesting than anything he would ever find in a toy store.

Mother went back to looking at a gold necklace, and asked Father if he thought she would look good in it.

Percival continued, "This game is a quest. We both look for things in the museum that begin with the letters of the alphabet. The only rule is that you can't find more than one letter in a single piece of art, and once a letter has been called out, it cannot be found again. When we have found all the letters from A to Z, the game is over."

"How do you know if you've won the game?" asked William.

"Simple!" said Percival. "Whoever finds the most letters wins. Are you ready?"

"Of course! But we won't find any in this wing" the boy said.

"On the contrary, we've already passed one. The letter M. M-M-Mummy, just as you entered."

"Rats! You're right—that's one for you." William and Percival followed Mother, Father and the baby through the exhibit.

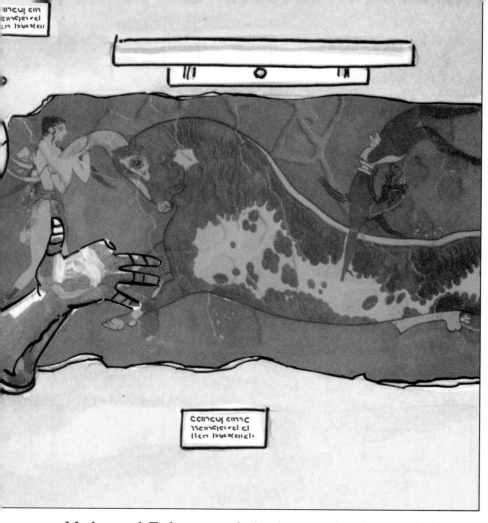

Mother and Father moved slowly, stopping here and there to view a sculpture or read a descriptive placard. William was eager to keep moving, his eyes darting about like a busy bee. Suddenly he blurted out, "Look, J-J-Jar! The Letter J—our score is even."

"Good catch, William!" said Percival. He lifted his visor and leaned forward to look at the jar, even though he had no face and no eyes. "It is very difficult to find the letter J. Now, over there you can see a portion of a wall from Knossos. On it, if I'm not mistaken are bull leapers. And where there are leapers, one finds a B-B-Bull. The Letter B." And with that they passed on into the European wing of the museum.

"Will my parents see you if you go in this wing?" asked William.

"No, they won't," said Percival. "They may begin to think that

the museum has a very large collection of old suits of armor."

This next wing of the museum was airy and bright, with an ornate archway that had come from Europe. Every wall was covered with paintings, many of which had huge golden frames.

"William, look at this lovely painting of the ballet!" Mother said. She was surprised when he came up and looked closely at the painting.

"Those are D-D-Dancers," said the boy, "The letter D."

"And over here is the letter G. G-G-Goat." mentioned the suit of armor. "I'm ahead of you again—you'd better keep your eyes sharp if you want to catch up!"

"Look at this painting, son," said Father. "The placard says that the sower theme comes from one of Jesus' parables and the sun is a symbol for the Light of the world."

"Sun? S-S-Sun, the letter S!" William stopped to look at the painting, even though he wasn't allowed to get another letter from it.

"If you look closely at this painting over here, you will find the letter F. F-F-Fan" pointed out the suit of armor. "That painter's name is Rembrandt. He is famous for his use of light and many paintings of biblical scenes. Your baby sister seems to have found a piece by Dutch Reformed artist Albrecht Dürer very interesting." The boy turned to see what Mother and his sister were studying.

"The Letter R. R-R-Rabbit—you get the point for that one." William said, smiling. "I wouldn't have seen it if you hadn't pointed it out."

Percival found the next letter also. "Q-Q-Queen," he said, pointing a metal finger at a portrait of a rather regal woman in a fancy dress. "That queen's name was Anne of Cleaves. She was one of the unfortunate ladies that married Henry VIII. I used to rescue queens from dragons all the time, of course that was before they sent me to the museum."

"I'm sure you did," said William. At some other time he might have asked more questions, but he had just found the letter 'E' in E-E-Egg.

Continuing further into the European wing of the museum, the suit of armor found the letter 'U' in U-U-Umbrella, spotted the letter 'H' in H-H-Hat and the letter 'Y' in Y-Y-Yellow "The painting of sunflowers that I found the letter Y in is by the man who did the painting where you found the letter S." instructed the hollow and quite metallic art historian. "The paintings in which Umbrella, Hat

and Yellow were located are all from an art movement called Impressionism."

The boy quickly followed Percival's discoveries with the letter W. "W-W-Windmill," he exclaimed. He was starting to get good at this game. Turning the corner, Willaim called back to Percival, "I found the letter 'T' over here!"

"So you did!" encouraged Percival. "This painting is of Jesus eating supper in Emmaus right before he disappeared, sitting at a table— T-T-Table."

Then William stopped in front of a large picture of the Roman colosseum and said, "L-L-Lion and the letter 'P,' in P-P-Pray. The Christians are praying before they get eaten."

"No," said Percival, "Remember the rule—one letter per painting. Which letter will you take?"

William thought for a moment. "I'll take the letter 'L' for Lion. I'm sure I can find 'P' before you can," he said laughing. "Come on—there's another part of the museum over here!"

The family passed through the archway into the American wing of the museum and as soon as they entered, William smiled broadly. "What an amazing pig! Hey, that is my letter P. P-P-Pig. I told you I would find 'P' soon."

As soon as Percival had made it under the archway he discovered the next letter. "And over here we have a painting of an Indian boy. The letter I, I-I-Indian. I don't think that he looks much older than we are, do you?"

The boy's father turned and asked his son, "Wasn't there a suit of armor on display just like that in the other wing of the museum?"

"You're right," said mother. "This museum does seem to have an awful lot of them."

"Perhaps this suit of armor walks from room to room and is following us," William suggested to his parents.

"Sure, son," William's father laughed. "And I bet the Assyrian lions protect the museum from burglars!"

Even though Percival had no body, and therefore no eyes, William could have sworn he saw Percival wink. Once William's parents had returned to enjoying the paintings on display, the suit of armor directed the boy's attention to a painting of a boxing match. "Do you hear the sound of 'X' in the word 'boxing'?" Percival asked the boy.

"Yes, I suppose we aren't going to find any other things in the museum in which we can find an 'X'" William replied.

"Since it didn't start the word, I won't take a point for that letter. Speaking of tallies, our score is ten to eight in my favor," Percival reported.

Then another painting caught William's eye, "Oo! Over there is a painting with apples in it. A-A-Apples, the Letter 'A'."

"I imagine we will find a great deal of our alphabet in this wing of the museum" mused the suit of armor. Percival jarred and jangled across the room to a black and white image, "This is an unpublished illustration by a doctor who wasn't a doctor who wrote about many things including birthday birds, bustard birds, sock-wearing foxes, green breakfast foods, an elephant with extraordinary hearing and a cat that wore hats. This is a picture he drew of three K-K-Kangaroos, the letter 'K'."

"To the right of the kangaroos is a painting of N-N-Nuts. They look so real, don't you feel like you could pick some right up off the surface of the canvas?" asked Percival. "That kind of painting is called *trompe l'oeil*. Here's another one. It depicts a V-V-Violin," the metal art critic continued.

William wasted no time in finding his next letter. "There is a cowboy! C-C-Cowboy is the letter C," he said triumphantly.

"No honey, actually that is an ox driver," said Mother.

"Really? Oh well, I can use it anyway. O-O-Ox, the letter 'O'. Oo! Look I found the last letter of the alphabet, too. This nineteenth century illustration is of a Z-Z-Zebra, the letter Z. Wow, that is twenty-five letters out of twenty-six. Do you think that we will find the last letter in the wing that houses the Special Exhibits?"

"Just be patient, we haven't finished the American art wing yet" the suit of armor cautioned.

William looked around, and saw several objects—but they were all letters that he had used before. "Percival, I can't remember. What letter is still left to find?" he asked.

"C-C-Cow," gurgled the boy's younger sister while pointing at a rustic painting. The boy laughed and said, "The letter C! Well, the game's over. Do you remember the score?"

Even though there was nothing inside the suit of armor, Percival seemed to blush. "Since your sister was wise enough to find the last letter, why don't we declare her the winner. Remember, the fun of the game is in the playing."

"The Alphabet Quest was a great game, Percival. Thank you so much. I'll never say that a museum is boring ever again."

Just then they heard a guard say that the museum would be closing in fifteen minutes. William thanked Percival yet again. "You have certainly helped me to look at museums in a whole new way. I can't wait to come back and see what else I can find."

"And I can't wait to play our next game," said Percival. He waved goodbye as the family walked towards the exit. Just as they walked out the door, William turned and waved back.

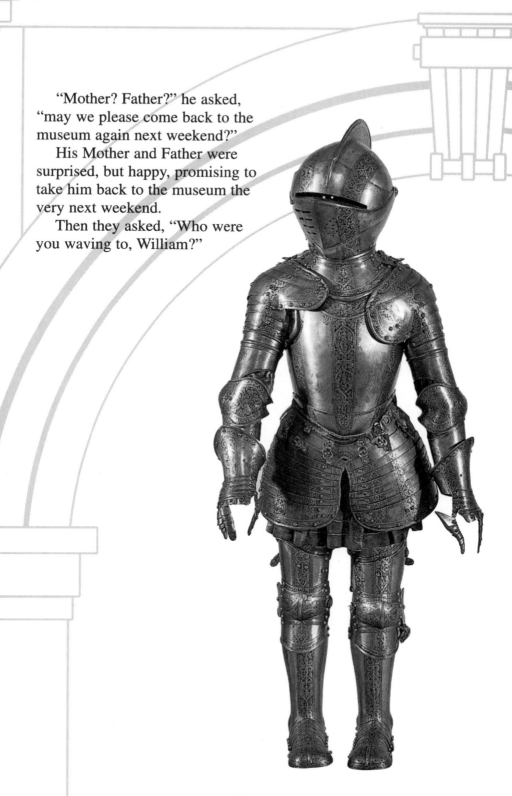

"Mother? Father?" he asked, "may we please come back to the museum again next weekend?"

His Mother and Father were surprised, but happy, promising to take him back to the museum the very next weekend.

Then they asked, "Who were you waving to, William?"

The following images for this book were taken from the collections of the Walters Art Gallery and the Brandywine River Museum—both excellent places to play the Alphabet Quest!

BRANDYWINE RIVER MUSEUM, CHADDS FORD, PA:

PAGE 25
Portrait of Pig by James Wyeth, ©1970 James Wyeth
Collection of the Brandywine River Museum, Gift of Betsy James Wyeth

PAGE 26
Apple Harvest by Levi Wells Prentice
Collection of the Brandywine River Museum, Museum Volunteers'
Purchase Fund, 1991

PAGE 27
"Good Gracious, Matilda—You Too?" by Theodore Seuss Geisel
Collection of the Brandywine River Museum, Gift of Jane Collette Wilcox

PAGE 27
Free Sample—Try One by De Scott Evans
Collection of the Brandywine River Museum, Museum Volunteers'
Purchase Fund, 1984

PAGE 28
The Ox Driver, an Old Time Figure of the West by Harvey Dunn
Collection of the Brandywine River Museum, Gift of Betsey Jacoby

THE WALTERS ART GALLERY:

PAGE 3, 5, 7, 8, 30 AND 31
Child's Suit of Armor German 16th century style

PAGE 19
Easter Egg by Karl Fabergé

PAGE 23
The Christian Martyr's Last Prayer by Jean-Léon Gérôme